UNE VIE DE CHIEN

IT'S A DOG'S LIFE

E.M
SPRADBERY

Matador
9 Priory Business Park,
Wistow Road, Kibworth Beauchamp,
Leicestershire. LE8 0RX
Tel: 0116 279 2299
Email: books@troubador.co.uk
Web: www.troubador.co.uk/matador
Twitter: @matadorbooks

ISBN 978 1785893 841

British Library Cataloguing in Publication Data.
A catalogue record for this book is available from the British Library.

Typeset in 12pt Barmeno by Troubador Publishing Ltd, Leicester, UK

Matador is an imprint of Troubador Publishing Ltd

Une Vie de Chien

This book is dedicated to my dear friend, Andrée, mother of Odile, now also a dear friend, and the talented illustrator of this volume.

With patience and proper training, man can learn to be a dog's best friend : Avec de la patience et de l'entraînement, l'homme peut apprendre à devenir le meilleur ami du chien

Foreword

Nine years ago my friend, Caroline, and I were travelling on a Eurostar train to Avignon, in the south of France, when it ran over a small tree on the line, and ground to a halt for several hours. I lent Andrée my mobile telephone to contact her husband in Avignon, and we have been friends ever since. Meeting in London and the south of France, and the south coast of England, too.

And so it was that one of the worst days of my life (I refer to the nightmare journey and not to our meeting!) led, eventually, to one of the best days (the acceptance of this book for publication).

I more recently met Odile, and another (VIP) important member of the family, Chloe, the beloved dog.

Odile and I, and Andrée too, all love animals in general and dogs in particular. And I must add Joey and Holly, my cats. So gradually the idea dawned on us that French phrases about animals would lend themselves well to Odile's great talent for drawing animals. Her website is: **www.bellucine.com**

1. Acheter chat en poche (literally: To buy a cat in a sack): To buy a pig in a poke
2. Chassez le naturel, il revient au galop (literally: Chase off what comes naturally, and it will return at a gallop): The leopard cannot change its spots
3. Un vieux sage hibou (literally: An old well-behaved owl): A wise old owl
4. Il y a anguille sous roche (literally: There is an eel under rock): There's something in the wind/ There's something fishy going on/I smell a rat
5. Comme un éléphant dans un magasin de porcelaine (literally: Like an elephant in a shop for china): Like a bull in a china shop

C'est un dur à cuire : He's a tough nut to crack

Qui se ressemble s'assemble : Birds of a feather flock together

6. Être comme l'âne de Buridan (literally: To be like Buridan's ass): To be unable to decide between two alternatives [A 14th century text, supposedly written by Buridan, tells of an ass who starves to death because he cannot choose between two identical piles of oats]

7. Le bonnet d'âne (literally: The hat of an ass): The dunce's cap

8. Faire l'âne pour avoir du son (literally: To act like an ass to get one's oats) : To play dumb to find out what one wants to know

9. C'est le pont aux ânes (literally: It's the bridge for asses): Any fool knows that!

10. Quand le chat n'est pas là, les souris dansent (literally: When the cat is not there, the mice dance): When the cat's away the mice will play

11. Changer un cheval borgne pour un aveugle (literally: To exchange a one-eyed horse for a blind one): Out of the frying pan into the fire

12. Ne changez pas de cheval au milieu du gué (literally: Don't change horses in the middle of the ford): Don't change horses midstream

13. L'argent ne se trouve pas sous le sabot d'un cheval (literally: Money is not found under the hoof of a horse): Money doesn't grow on trees

14. Monter sur ses grands chevaux (literally: To mount one's big horses): To get on one's high horse

15. Arriver comme un chien dans un jeu de quilles (literally: To arrive like a dog in a games of skittles): To turn up when least needed or wanted

16. Avaler des couleuvres (literally: To swallow snakes): To swallow an affront, to be taken in, to swallow anything; to eat up the kilometres/miles

Un dîner de fous : Out to lunch

3

Il fait un froid de canard : It's freezing cold

17. Ils se sont regardés en chiens de faïence (literally: They looked at each other like china dogs): They sat glaring at each other
18. C'est le serpent qui se mord la queue (literally: It's the snake that bites its tail): It's a vicious circle
19. Un serpent de mer (literally: a snake of the sea): A trite news story [to fall back on in the absence of more important news]
20. Si les petits cochons ne te mangent pas (literally: If the little pigs don't eat you): If the bogeyman doesn't get you
21. (Et) cochon qui s'en dédit (literally: (And) a pig anyone who defaults [on the deal]: Let's shake (hands) on it
22. Être à cheval sur ses principes (literally: To be on horseback astride one's principles): To be a stickler for principles

23. C'est un vieux renard (literally: It's an old fox): He's a sly old dog
24. Un passage clouté (literally: a studded way): A zebra/pedestrian crossing [And a pelican crossing is a pedestrian crossing at traffic lights operated by pedestrians]
25. Faire ça ou peigner la girafe (literally: Do this or comb the giraffe): It's either that or some other pointless task
26. Noyer le poisson (literally: To drown the fish): To evade the issue, to sidestep the question
27. Dormir comme un loir (literally: To sleep like a dormouse): To sleep like a log
28. La mare aux harengs (literally: the Herring Pond – humorous): The North Atlantic

**Comme un oiseau sur la branche :
Here today and gone tomorrow**

Entre chien et loup : At dusk

29. Le vilain petit canard (literally: The ugly little duck):
The Ugly Duckling
30. Parler français comme une vache espagnole
(literally: To speak French like a Spanish cow): To
murder the French language
31. Les chiens aboient, la caravane passe (literally: The
dogs bark, the procession passes): Let the world
say what it will
32. Un rat de bibliothèque (literally: A library rat): A
bookworm
33. On n'apprend pas à un vieux singe à faire des
grimaces (literally: You can't teach an old monkey
to make grimaces/to pull faces): Don't teach your
grandmother to suck eggs

34. Il est malin comme un singe (literally: He is crafty like a monkey) He's a sly old devil

35. Payer quelqu'un en monnaie de singe (literally: To pay somebody in monkey money): To fob somebody off with empty promises

36. Abandonner quelqu'un à son sort (literally: To abandon somebody to their fate): To throw somebody to the dogs

37. Il joue l'empêcheur de tourner en rond (literally: He plays at blocking people from going round and round): He's being a dog in the manger

38. S'entendre comme chien et chat (literally: To understand each other like dog and cat): To fight like cat and dog

Le loup retourne toujours au bois :
One always goes back to one's roots

Ne réveillez pas le chat qui dort :
Let sleeping dogs lie

39. Ce n'est pas à son âge qu'on apprend de nouveaux trucs (literally: It's not at his age that you learn new things): You can't teach an old dog new tricks

40. Coiffée à la chien (literally: With hair dressed in the style of a dog): To wear a fringe

41. Je ne suis pas ton chien (literally: I am not your dog): I'm not your slave

42. Bon chien chasse de race (literally: Good dog, as befits the pedigree): Like father like son

43. Marcher à la ruine (literally: To walk to[wards] ruination): To go to the dogs

44. À chacun son tour (literally: To each his turn): Every dog has his day

45. Se jeter dans la gueule du loup (literally: To throw oneself into the wolf's mouth): To rush into the lion's mouth

46. Marcher à pas de loup (literally: To walk with the steps of a wolf): To walk stealthily, to creep along

Revenons à nos moutons :
Let's get back to the subject

47. Tenir le loup par les oreilles (literally: To hold the wolf by his ears): To be in a fix

48. Quand on parle du loup on en voit la queue (literally: When you speak about a wolf you can see his tail): Talk of the devil, and he appears

49. Les loups ne se mangent pas entre eux (literally: Wolves won't eat each other): A thief won't snitch on a thief

50. À bon chat bon rat (literally: For a good cat a good rat): Tit for tat

51. Il a une araignée au plafond (literally: He has a spider on his ceiling):   He's got bats in the belfry

52. Il se fait prendre pour un pigeon (literally: He makes himself be taken for a pigeon): He is taken for a ride

Faire le singe : To monkey about

53. Vendre la peau de l'ours avant de l'avoir tué
    (literally: To sell the bear's skin before having killed
    it): To count your chickens before they are hatched

54. Avoir le cafard (literally: To have the cockroach):
    To feel blue, to be down in the dumps

55. Se coucher avec les poules (literally: To go to bed
    with the hens): To go to bed early

56. Sortir de la gueule d'une vache (literally: To come out
    of the mouth of a cow): To be creased (a garment)

57. Faire le pied de grue (literally: To do/make the foot
    of a crane): To hang around waiting

Il pleut des cordes : It's raining cats and dogs

58. Donner sa langue au chat (literally: To give one's tongue to the cat): To give up, not to know
59. Avoir des fourmis dans les bras (literally: To have ants in your arms): To have pins and needles in your arm
60. Il n'y a pas de lézard (literally: There is no lizard there): Not a problem
61. Tirer les vers du nez de quelqu'un (literally: To pull worms from somebody's nose): To worm information out of somebody

62. Avoir des oursins dans les poches (literally: To have sea urchins in your pocket): To be stingy

63. Décoiffer la girafe (literally: To mess up the hair of a giraffe): To do something difficult

64. Pratiquer la politique de l'autruche (literally: To practise the politics of the ostrich): To bury one's head in the sand

65. Jeter un pavé dans la mare (literally: To throw a cobblestone into the pond): To set the cat among the pigeons

66. Un loup déguisé en agneau (literally: A wolf disguised as a sheep): A wolf in sheep's clothing

67. Mettre le loup dans la bergerie (literally: To put the wolf into the sheepfold): To set the fox to mind the geese

68. Vendre la mèche : (Literally: To sell the wick): To let the cat out of the bag, to spill the beans

Se lever au chant du coq :
To rise with the lark

F<small>IN</small> – <small>END</small>

Lightning Source UK Ltd.
Milton Keynes UK
UKHW021336271018
331313UK00003B/25/P

9 781785 893841